THE TRANSCONTINENTAL RAILROAD

A PRIMARY SOURCE HISTORY OF AMERICA'S FIRST COAST-TO-COAST RAILROAD

GILLIAN HOUGHTON

rosen central
Primary Source

For Jason

Published in 2003 by The Rosen Publishing Group, Inc.
29 East 21st Street, New York, NY 10010

Library of Congress Cataloging-in-Publication Data

Houghton, Gillian.
The Transcontinental Railroad: A Primary Source History of America's First Coast-to-Coast Railroad / Gillian Houghton.
   p. cm. — (Primary sources in American history)
Summary: Describes the people, circumstances, and events surrounding the building of the railway system across the continent in the mid-nineteenth century.
ISBN 0-8239-3684-8 (library binding)
1. Railroads—United States—History—Juvenile literature. 2. Union Pacific Railroad Company—History—Juvenile literature. 3. Central Pacific Railroad Company—History—Juvenile literature. [1. Railroads–West (U.S.)—History. 2. Union Pacific Railroad Company—History. 3. Central Pacific Railroad Company—History.]
I. Title. II. Series.
TF25.U5 H68 2003
385'.0973'09034—dc21

                                                                    2001008530

Manufactured in the United States of America

CONTENTS

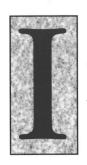NTRODUCTION

RAILROAD BEGINNINGS

In his book *Nothing Like It in the World: The Men Who Built the Transcontinental Railroad*, historian Stephen Ambrose reports that in 1867, as the first transcontinental railroad entered its third year of construction, Arthur Ferguson, a surveyor for the Union Pacific Railroad Company, made this observation: "The time is coming and fast too, when in the sense it is now understood, there will be no west." In many ways, history would prove Ferguson correct.

The completion of the transcontinental railroad meant that coast-to-coast travel and communication would be possible. The railroad would connect what were once widely scattered and isolated settlements west of the Mississippi River. Scientific discoveries, cultural events, and political ideas could be reported instantaneously over telegraph wires, which were erected beside the track bed as the rails were laid. Magazines, books, and other products could be distributed by rail to a new national audience. The railroad would spur the growth of national corporations and, as a result, make the creation of a national stock exchange possible.

Despite these advances, the story of the transcontinental railroad is a tale of pride, greed, discrimination, and violence. The surveyors, engineers, and businessmen who led the railroad companies took advantage of immigrant laborers. They bribed and cheated the U.S. government. They nearly destroyed the Sioux and Cheyenne Indian tribes, and they contributed to the near extinction of the American buffalo. They believed in manifest destiny, which means they thought it was their right and obligation to settle the country west of the Mississippi River. In the beginning of the nineteenth century, America was waiting to be explored, and several thousand adventurous men accepted the challenge. As they stretched the rails in every direction, the railroad moguls of the nineteenth century changed the face of America forever.

TIMELINE

1848 —— Gold is discovered in the mining fields forty miles west of Sacramento, California.

1853 —— The United States Congress sponsors an expedition of surveyors to document the lands west of the Mississippi and to suggest possible routes for a transcontinental railroad.

1856 —— Funded by Thomas Durant and George Francis Train, General Grenville Dodge begins a surveying expedition and determines that the Platte Valley route is the best route for a transcontinental railroad.

1861 —— Abraham Lincoln is inaugurated president of the United States; in response, the thirteen states of the Confederacy secede from the Union, and the American Civil War begins.

June 28, 1861 — The Central Pacific Railroad Company is organized, with Leland Stanford as president.

1862 —— The Homestead Act (which granted every United States citizen the right to claim 160 acres of land in the western frontier) is ratified by Congress.

TIMELINE

July 1, 1862 — President Lincoln signs the Pacific Railroad Act, which creates the Union Pacific Railroad Company under the authority of a board of directors chosen by Congress.

January 8, 1863 — The Central Pacific breaks ground on Front and K Streets in Sacramento, California.

November 2, 1863 — Theodore Judah, the chief engineer of the Union Pacific Railroad Company, dies in New York after having contracted yellow fever in Panama.

April 1865 — President Lincoln is assassinated; two weeks later, the South surrenders, ending the Civil War.

November 30, 1867 — The first Central Pacific train rides the rails through the Summit Tunnel, the longest and most elevated tunnel on the Central Pacific line.

January 9, 1869 — The Union Pacific lays its 1,000th mile of track west of Omaha, Nebraska.

May 10, 1869 — The last spike is hammered into the rails joining the Union Pacific and Central Pacific Railroads in Promontory Summit, Utah.

CHAPTER 1

PICKING THE ROUTE

By 1846, the United States had extended its territorial boundaries to the Pacific Ocean in the West, the forty-ninth latitude in the North, and Mexico in the South. This wild but fertile frontier was virtually uninhabited by white settlers, with the exception of fur traders and gold miners. Then, in 1848, a phenomenal lode of gold was discovered about forty miles west of Sacramento, California. The promise of riches hidden in the foothills of the Sierra Nevada had come true; there was gold in the mountains. In only a few years, dozens of settlements dotted the West Coast. Young men from the East risked their savings and their lives to test their luck in the California wilderness. In 1850 alone, 55,000 men began the journey to California. By 1860, more than 300,000 men (and a small group of women) had traveled west with dreams of striking it rich.

There were three ways to get from New York and other industrialized cities in the East to the booming gold mining towns of

This 1849 advertisement appeared in the *Rochester Daily Advertiser*. The speaker, W. R. Andrews, promises to exhibit gold dust, chunks of gold, and models of the machines used to mine and process the gold. At the bottom of the broadside (as these large posters or printed advertisements were called), Andrews printed a letter signed by passengers aboard the *Panama*, the boat that he had sailed on from San Francisco to New York. The letter is a testimonial from these fellow travelers in support of Andrews.

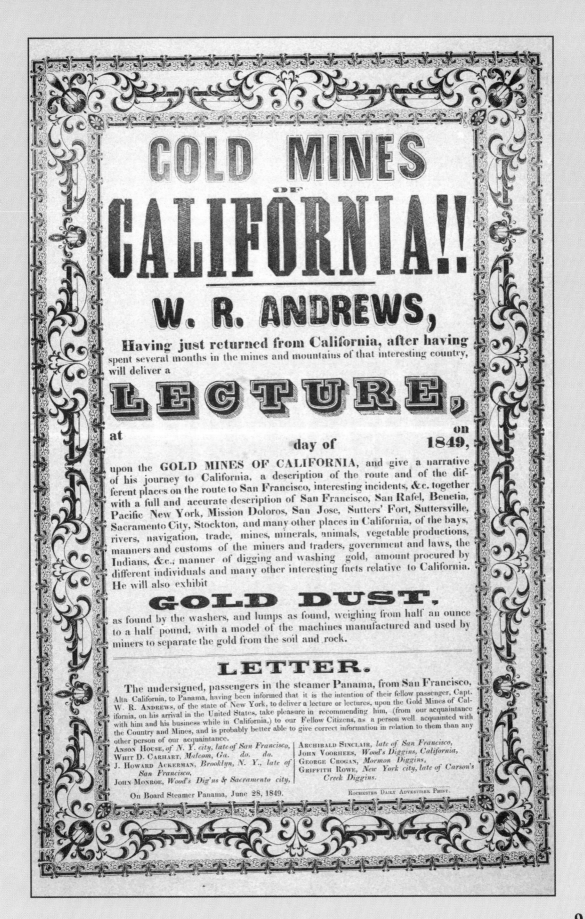

GOLD MINES OF CALIFORNIA!!

W. R. ANDREWS,

Having just returned from California, after having spent several months in the mines and mountains of that interesting country, will deliver a

LECTURE,

at   day of   1849,   on

upon the GOLD MINES OF CALIFORNIA, and give a narrative of his journey to California, a description of the route and of the different places on the route to San Francisco, interesting incidents, &c. together with a full and accurate description of San Francisco, San Rafel, Benetia, Pacific New York, Mission Doloros, San Jose, Sutters' Fort, Suttersville, Sacramento City, Stockton, and many other places in California, of the bays, rivers, navigation, trade, mines, minerals, animals, vegetable productions, manners and customs of the miners and traders, government and laws, the Indians, &c.; manner of digging and washing gold, amount procured by different individuals and many other interesting facts relative to California. He will also exhibit

GOLD DUST.

as found by the washers, and lumps as found, weighing from half an ounce to a half pound, with a model of the machines manufactured and used by miners to separate the gold from the soil and rock.

LETTER.

The undersigned, passengers in the steamer Panama, from San Francisco, Alta California, to Panama, having been informed that it is the intention of their fellow passenger, Capt. W. R. ANDREWS, of the state of New York, to deliver a lecture or lectures, upon the Gold Mines of California, on his arrival in the United States, take pleasure in recommending him, (from our acquaintance with him and his business while in California,) to our Fellow Citizens, as a person well acquainted with the Country and Mines, and is probably better able to give correct information in relation to them than any other person of our acquaintance.

ANSON HOUSE, *of N. Y. city, late of San Francisco,*
WHIT D. CARHART, *Malcom, Ga. do. do.*
J. HOWARD ACKERMAN, *Brooklyn, N. Y., late of San Francisco,*
JOHN MONROE, *Wood's Dig'ns & Sacramento city,*

ARCHIBALD SINCLAIR, *late of San Francisco,*
JOHN VOORHEES, *Wood's Diggins, California,*
GEORGE CROGAN, *Mormon Diggins,*
GRIFFITH ROWE, *New York city, late of Carson's Creek Diggins.*

On Board Steamer Panama, June 28, 1849.

ROCHESTER DAILY ADVERTISER PRINT.

California and Nevada. A traveler could take the train to Omaha, Nebraska, and then board a stagecoach bound for the treacherous mountain paths of the Rocky Mountains and Sierra Nevada. If wild animals or bands of Sioux or Cheyenne didn't raid the coach along the way, a traveler might arrive safely at his or her destination.

A second alternative was to sail around Cape Horn, the southern tip of South America, on a crowded, expensive schooner. After arriving in San Francisco or Sacramento, the traveler would take a wagon or stagecoach to his or her destination. A final option was to travel by ship to the Isthmus of Panama in Central America, travel on foot or by coach over land, and sail from the western coast of Panama to California. In fair weather, the trip over land through the United States could take more than six months. Ships bound for Cape Horn were often robbed by pirates and burned at sea. Travelers across the Isthmus of Panama nearly always got sick.

Broadsides like W. R. Andrews's were printed in newspapers and distributed in towns. People were anxious for as much information about the vast western wilderness as possible. Andrews promised details of "the bays, rivers, navigation, trade, mines, minerals, animals, vegetable productions . . . Indians, &c. manner of digging and washing gold, amount procured by different individuals and many other interesting facts relative to California." In other words, Andrews claimed to offer everything an adventurer would need to know to get started.

Because the trip to California by stagecoach or boat was very difficult, people soon looked to the railroads to provide safe, fast overland travel. The first steam-powered boats navigated the Mississippi River in 1807, but it wasn't until nearly two decades later that the technology involved in harnessing steam power was applied to the locomotive.

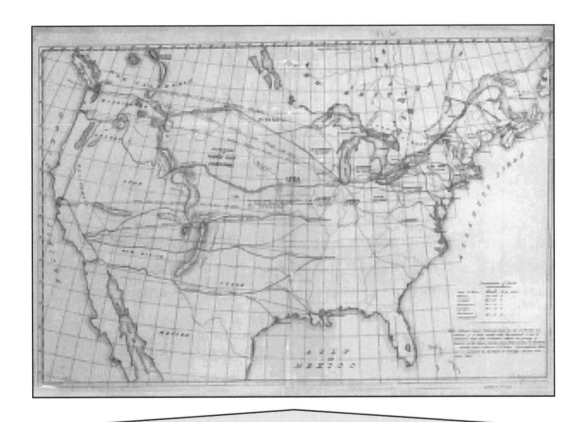

Many surveyors joined the search for the best railroad route to the West. This map, published in 1853 by surveyor William Jarvis McAlpine, illustrates several possible routes for the first transcontinental railroad. McAlpine's recommendation for a central route running west from the Missouri River mirrors the route chosen by Abraham Lincoln, until McAlpine's survey reaches the Rocky Mountains, at which point it heads north. In doing so, McAlpine avoids the treacherous Sierra Nevada. Further north, McAlpine's route joins the proposed northern route from St. Paul, Minnesota, to Seattle, in the Washington Territory.

These early trains were dirty, dangerous, and slow. They belched out thick columns of smoke that drifted downwind of the tracks. Passengers spent the bumpy ride perched uncomfortably on uneven, backless benches. Each car had a separate brake, which had to be pulled by hand, making emergency or unexpected stops

This portrait of Major General Grenville M. Dodge of the Federal (or Union) army was taken in the early 1860s. During the Civil War, Dodge commanded troops and was responsible for building and maintaining the railroads across the Northeast that supplied Union troops. He was a legendary commander and engineer. In 1864, during a visit to the battlefront in Atlanta, Georgia, he was shot in the head. He survived, but he was forced to leave the front lines and head west. Dodge was assigned to the Department of the Missouri, where his duties included protecting western settlers and railroad employees from Indians, including the Sioux and Cheyenne, who were attempting to defend their lives, their land, and their way of life. He commanded with an iron fist, killing and imprisoning entire Indian communities before joining the Union Pacific Railroad Company in 1866.

impossible. Discomfort aside, to the traveler of the mid-nineteenth century, these trains were powerful iron horses (as new trains came to be called). It became clear to railroad investors, the government, and the public at large that the best way to exploit the natural resources of the West and protect the new settlements of the frontier was to build an iron road that connected the East and West. The railroads could carry lumber and other raw materials to the factories in the East and transport army troops from their homes in the East to the isolated forts in the West.

The prospect of a coast-to-coast railroad was met with much enthusiasm. Newspaper editorials and railroad journals applauded the idea, politicians demanded it, and a few enterprising surveyors went into the wilderness to look for the best route for the railroad to follow. This was a courageous feat. Surveyors had to learn the ins and outs of thousands of square miles of land inhabited by Indians and wild animals. Their equipment was often limited to a compass, a level, and a pack mule.

In 1853, Congress authorized government-sponsored explorations—known as the Pacific Railroad Surveys—under the supervision of Secretary of War Jefferson Davis. Five possible routes were determined, and the surveyors presented their reports to Congress in twelve volumes. The northern route followed the forty-seventh latitude from St. Paul, Minnesota, to Seattle, in the Washington Territory. The central route ran along the Platte River Valley, from Omaha, Nebraska, to San Francisco, California. A third route, called the Buffalo Trail, ran through the Colorado Territory. Two southern routes ran through the New Mexico and Arizona Territories to southern California. Eventually, trains would travel each of these paths, and modern engineers would make few improvements on the original routes. In 1853, however, political, economic, and social divisions between the southern and northern states prevented Congress from choosing a route. Even as Congress sat stalled during the following decade, surveyors headed west. One such surveyor was Grenville Dodge.

Grenville Dodge was born in Massachusetts on April 12, 1831. He began working for the railroad at the age of fourteen. After studying engineering at Norwich University in Vermont, he moved to Illinois, where the railroad revolution was beginning. Dodge was eager and strong-willed, and he had ambitious plans for the future of the railways. In 1856, funded by Wall Street businessman Dr. Thomas Durant and railroad investor Henry Farnam, Dodge led an expedition to survey the Platte Valley route.

The land west of the Missouri River was a great expanse of flat, dusty plains, rolling hills, river valleys, and sheltering woods leading to the foothills of the Rocky Mountains. Long before Dodge began his surveys, each year the Cheyenne and Sioux had followed the buffalo herds along the Platte Valley route. The same path was taken by the Rocky Mountains fur-trading companies and, after them, by a group of religious exiles from the East and Midwest known as the Mormons, who were on their way to a new settlement in the wilderness of Utah. The route was ideal for travel by foot or by rail; the river provided a source of freshwater, and the flat land was easy to navigate in a straight, level line.

When Dodge completed his initial surveys, he traveled to New York City to meet with the directors of Durant's investment company and to present his plans for a railroad along the Platte River. By the end of the meeting, the only people left in the room were Grenville Dodge, Thomas Durant, and Henry Farnam; the other businessmen had left in disbelief. The three remaining men were the only ones who believed the project could be done.

The National Republican Convention was held in Chicago, Illinois, on May 17, 1860. Grenville Dodge and several other representatives of the railroads attended the convention in support of Abraham Lincoln, a longtime supporter of the expansion of the railroads. Lincoln's election was critical if a national railroad was to be built. It was on the issue of slavery, however, that this platform was adopted and Abraham Lincoln was chosen as the Republican nominee for the presidency of the United States. See pages 55–57 for transcription.

NATIONAL REPUBLICAN

PLATFORM

ADOPTED BY THE

NATIONAL REPUBLICAN CONVENTION,

HELD IN CHICAGO, MAY 17, 1860.

Resolved, That we, the delegated representatives of the Republican electors of the United States, in Convention assembled, in discharge of the duty we owe to our constituents and our country, unite in the following declarations:

The Republican Party.

1. That the history of the nation during the last four years, has fully established the propriety and necessity of the organization and perpetuation of the Republican party, and that the causes which called it into existence are permanent in their nature, and now, more than ever before, demand its peaceful and constitutional triumph.

Its Fundamental Principles.

2. That the maintenance of the principles promulgated in the Declaration of Independence and embodied in the Federal Constitution, "That all men are created equal; that they are endowed by their Creator with certain inalienable rights; that among these are life, liberty, and the pursuit of happiness; that to secure these rights, governments are instituted among men, deriving their just powers from the consent of the governed," is essential to the preservation of our Republican institutions; and that the Federal Constitution, the Rights of the States, and the Union of the States, must and shall be preserved.

[ ] to the Union.

3. That to the Union of the States, this nation owes its unprecedented increase of population, its surprising development of material resources, its rapid augmentation of wealth, its happiness at home and its honor abroad; and we hold in abhorrence all schemes for Disunion, come from whatever source they may: And we congratulate the country, that no Republican member of Congress has uttered or countenanced the threats of Disunion so often made by Democratic members, without rebuke and with applause from their political associates; and we denounce those threats of Disunion, in case of a popular overthrow of their ascendancy as denying the vital principles of a free government, and as an avowal of contemplated treason, which it is the imperative duty of an indignant People sternly to rebuke and forever silence.

State Sovereignty.

4. That the maintenance inviolate of the Rights of the States, and especially the right of each State to order and control its own domestic institutions according to its own judgment exclusively, is essential to that balance of power on which the perfection and endurance of our political fabric depends; and we denounce the lawless invasion by armed force of the soil of any State or Territory, no matter under what pretext, as among the gravest of crimes.

Sectionalism of the Democracy.

5. That the present Democratic Administration has far exceeded our worst apprehensions, in its measureless subserviency to the exactions of a sectional interest, as especially evinced in its desperate exertions to force the infamous Lecompton Constitution upon the protesting people of Kansas; in construing the personal relation between master and servant to involve an unqualified property in persons; in its attempted enforcement, everywhere, on land and sea, through the intervention of Congress and of the Federal Courts, of the extreme pretensions of a purely local interest; and in its general and unvarying abuse of power entrusted to it by a confiding people.

Its Extravagance and Corruption.

6. That the people justly view with alarm the reckless extravagance which pervades every department of the Federal Government; that a return to rigid economy and accountability is indispensable to arrest the systematic plunder of the public treasury by favored partisans; while the recent startling developments of frauds and corruptions at the Federal metropolis, show that an entire change of administration is imperatively demanded.

A Dangerous Political Heresy.

7. That the new dogma that the Constitution, of its own force, carries Slavery into any or all of the Territories of the United States, is a dangerous political heresy, at variance with the explicit provisions of that instrument itself, with contemporaneous exposition, and with legislative and judicial precedent; is revolutionary in its tendency, and subversive of the peace and harmony of the country.

Freedom, the Normal Condition of Territories.

8. That the normal condition of all the territory of the United States is that of Freedom: That as our Republican fathers, when they had abolished slavery in all our national territory, ordained that "no person should be deprived of life, liberty, or property, without due process of law," it becomes our duty, by legislation, whenever such legislation is necessary, to maintain this provision of the Constitution against all attempts to violate it; and we deny the authority of Congress, of a territorial legislature, or of any individuals, to give legal existence to slavery in any Territory of the United States.

The African Slave Trade.

9. That we brand the recent re-opening of the African Slave Trade, under the cover of our national flag, aided by perversions of judicial power, as a crime against humanity and a burning shame to our country and age; and we call upon Congress to take prompt and efficient measures for the total and final suppression of that execrable traffic.

Democratic Popular Sovereignty.

10. That in the recent vetoes, by their Federal Governors of the acts of the Legislatures of Kansas and Nebraska, prohibiting Slavery in those Territories, we find a practical illustration of the boasted Democratic principle of Non-Intervention and Popular Sovereignty embodied in the Kansas-Nebraska Bill, and a demonstration of the deception and fraud involved therein.

Admission of Kansas.

11. That Kansas should, of right, be immediately admitted as a State under the Constitution recently formed and adopted by her people, and accepted by the House of Representatives.

Encouragement of American Industry.

12. That, while providing revenue for the support of the general government by duties upon imports, sound policy requires such an adjustment of these imports as to encourage the development of the industrial interests of the whole country; and we commend that policy of national exchanges, which secures to the working men liberal wages, to agriculture remunerating prices, to mechanics and manufacturers an adequate reward for their skill, labor and enterprise, and to the nation commercial prosperity and independence.

Free Homesteads.

13. That we protest against any sale or alienation to others of the Public Lands held by actual settlers, and against any view of the Free Homestead policy which regards the settlers as paupers or suppliants for public bounty; and we demand the passage by Congress of the complete and satisfactory Homestead Measure which has already passed the House.

Rights of Citizenship.

14. That the Republican party is opposed to any change in our Naturalization Laws or any State legislation by which the rights of citizenship hitherto accorded to immigrants from foreign lands shall be abridged or impaired; and in favor of giving a full and efficient protection to the rights of all classes of citizens, whether native or naturalized, both at home and abroad.

River and Harbor Improvements.

15. That appropriations by Congress for River and Harbor improvements of a National character, required for the accommodation and security of an existing commerce, are authorized by the Constitution, and justified by the obligation of Government to protect the lives and property of its citizens.

A Pacific Railroad.

16. That a Railroad to the Pacific Ocean is imperatively demanded by the interests of the whole country; that the Federal Government ought to render immediate and efficient aid in its construction; and that, as preliminary thereto, a daily Overland Mail should be promptly established.

Co-operation Invited.

17. Finally, having thus set forth our distinctive principles and views, we invite the co-operation of all citizens, however differing on other questions, who substantially agree with us in their affirmance and support.

Abraham Lincoln was a long-standing proponent of the railroad industry. During his terms as an Illinois state representative (1834–1842) and congressman (1847–1849), the Illinois Central Railroad grew steadily, soon exceeding in length any other railroad network in the world. In his campaign for the Republican nomination for the presidency of the United States, Lincoln advocated a railroad from coast to coast. The primary obstacle facing the construction of a transcontinental railroad was the issue of slavery. Secretary of War Jefferson Davis, who would go on to be the president of the Confederacy during the Civil War, argued for the southern route from New Orleans, Louisiana, to San Diego, California. This route would extend slavery by connecting southern slave states and the uncharted, unregulated western frontier. No free state would agree to the southern route. Likewise, the northerners wanted the railroad to begin in Chicago or St. Paul, but no southern politician would accept this.

At the 1860 Republican National Convention, delegates adopted one of the most important party platforms in American history. In it, the Republican Party described the slave trade as "a crime against humanity and a burning shame to our country and age." The party pledged to "call upon Congress to take prompt and efficient measures for the total and final suppression" of slavery in the United States. The following fall, Lincoln was elected president, in part on the strength of his antislavery message. To defend the institution of slavery and state sovereignty, thirteen southern states seceded from the Union. On April 12, 1861, the first shots of the American Civil War were fired at Fort Sumter in South Carolina.

The 1860 Republican platform also said that "a Railroad to the Pacific Ocean is imperatively demanded by the interests of the whole country" and that Congress should offer immediate aid for its construction. Instead of dampening America's enthusiasm for the railroads, the outbreak of war solved the problem of determining the iron horse's route. The Union Congress, now made up of only free-state politicians, faced no opposition in choosing a northern route. They immediately began debating and drafting a bill to organize and finance the construction of a transcontinental railroad along the Platte Valley route. On July 1, 1862, Lincoln signed the Pacific Railroad Act.

The Pacific Railroad Act provided financial incentives to corporations that undertook the construction of the railroad. Two corporations would rise to the task. The Central Pacific Railroad would build east from Sacramento, California, and the Union Pacific Railroad would build west from Omaha, Nebraska. They would meet at a town to be determined by Congress at a later date. The government would allot a certain number of acres of land on either side of the railroad for every mile of track that was laid. The railroad companies would build stations and warehouses on this valuable land or sell it to settlers to offset construction costs.

For each mile of track laid, the government would also give each railroad company a certain number of government bonds, which could also be sold for each company's profit. However, as Dodge discovered in his 1856 meeting with Durant and Farnam, many investors would be wary of the proposition. Building a railroad from coast to coast was a job for a remarkable man, one who was part engineer, part accountant, part wise man, part politician, and part swindler.

It would take not one but five men to rise to the challenge. The men of the Central Pacific Railroad Company were risk takers and adventurers who dreamed of being part of something monumental.

CHAPTER 2

THEODORE JUDAH AND THE BIG FOUR

Four men would create and lead the Central Pacific Railroad: Leland Stanford, Collis P. Huntington, Charles Crocker, and Mark Hopkins. Each man came to California on the heels of the "forty-niners"—the adventurous, would-be gold miners who flooded California in 1849. But it was a young Connecticut engineer named Theodore Judah who would offer these four men the business opportunity that would make them California legends. Judah was an experienced surveyor and engineer from the East Coast. In 1854, he moved his family from New York to Sacramento, California, to work on the first railroad west of the Mississippi River. The line ran from Sacramento to Folsom, California, just west of the Sierra Nevada, and it served the gold miners of Placerville, California.

Theodore Judah was the chief engineer of the Central Pacific Railroad. The immense project would not have been completed without Judah's courage, enthusiasm, and leadership. Not long after Judah created the company in 1861, however, the primary investors and board members nearly bankrupted it in an attempt to make fast money. Judah did not live to see the completion of the railroad and, in his short life, was consistently troubled by his greedy and irresponsible Central Pacific Railroad colleagues. This portrait of Judah dates from 1863.

Upon the railroad's completion in 1855, Judah dreamed of building something even bigger—a train line from coast to coast. Judah believed that a railroad of such size and expense would have to be sponsored by the government. While employed as chief engineer of the Sacramento Valley and the Sacramento Valley Central Railroads, Judah traveled to Washington, D.C., to promote a coast-to-coast railroad.

At his own expense, he published a promotional pamphlet that he distributed to every member of Congress, and he pitched his idea to anyone who would listen. Congress was deadlocked, or unable to make a decision by a majority; disagreements between free and slave states defeated all of Judah's endeavors in Washington. Disheartened, he returned to Sacramento. In 1859, a convention of local politicians and businessmen organized by the California legislature decided that the western terminus, or end, of the transcontinental railroad should be Sacramento, California. Judah was chosen by the group to relay the decision to Washington and to continue his efforts there at the expense of these local investors.

Later that year, Judah set up an office in Washington's capitol building that served as a mini-museum of his plans for a transcontinental railroad. Unlike Jefferson Davis's 1853 surveys, Judah's exhibits detailed the exact path of the line, how many cubic feet of earth would have to be moved to keep a level or gentle incline, and other specifics of laying track. Maps and mineral samples were carefully displayed. His surveys considered other factors, such as snow and foul weather, population, and the construction of locomotives. However, Judah's exhibits failed to explain how the railroad would cross the wide rivers, the Great Basin of Nevada, and, most important, the Sierra Nevada. In the summer of 1860, Judah returned to California in order to perform a detailed survey of the Sierra Nevada, to determine the line of the railroad track through this phenomenal mountain range, and to form the corporation that would build the railroad.

After countless cold nights sleeping on the ground, cooking meals over an open fire, hiking hundreds of miles, and scaling treacherous mountain passes in search of a route, the task was accomplished. At the suggestion of a pharmacist from Dutch Flat, California, named Daniel W. Strong, Judah surveyed Donner Pass and determined that it was the best route through the mountains for the railroad.

At Dr. Strong's store in Dutch Flat, Judah drew up the Articles of Association. It served as a preliminary outline of the organization of the company that would later become the Central Pacific Railroad. A month and a half later, Lincoln was elected president, and the dream of a railroad to Sacramento became a real possibility.

When Judah returned to Sacramento in November 1860, he held a series of open meetings at the St. Joseph Hotel. There, he presented his plan for a railroad spanning to the Sierra Nevada (and perhaps as far as the state line of Nevada) to a crowd of businessmen. His real goal was a coast-to-coast railroad, but in his presentation to potential investors, Judah scaled back his plans to avoid appearing fanatical or crazy.

Leland Stanford and three other Sacramento businessmen, Collis P. Huntington, Charles Crocker, and Mark Hopkins, were among the crowd at the St. Joseph one night and at a smaller meeting soon after, and they liked the idea. The railroad would connect their stores with the markets of the Nevada mining towns, and if they owned the railroad, they would set the price of transporting their goods. If a railroad over the mountains proved

Born into a family of seven brothers on a small farm in rural New York, Leland Stanford went on to become one of the most famous men in railroad history. Stanford practiced law in Port Washington, Wisconsin, from 1848 to 1852. In 1852, after his law office burned to the ground, Stanford headed west. He briefly worked as a miner before joining his brothers, who had moved to California in 1849, in business. The Stanfords were shopkeepers. When he had made a significant fortune, Stanford moved to Sacramento, where he opened a store of his own and entered state politics. This portrait was painted in 1880.

financially impossible, Judah argued, he would build the merchants a wagon road (a flat roadbed) east from Dutch Flat, from which they could expect huge profits by charging high tolls. The four men invested private money to fund a more complete survey of the route. Judah left for the mountains in the spring of 1861 to conduct this final survey.

On June 28, 1861, the Central Pacific Railroad was officially created, and Leland Stanford, who was about to be elected governor of California, was chosen as president of the company. Stanford would go on to become the third president of the Southern Pacific Company, the founder of Stanford University in Palo Alto, California, and the most famous of the Big Four, as the Sacramento store owners came to be called. He became an important figure in local and national government and was a close friend of Abraham Lincoln's. He had a reputation as a fair, friendly man who was often called upon to settle disputes between local miners and businessmen.

However, first and foremost, the Big Four were businessmen. They expected a profit from their investment in the Central Pacific, and they would do almost anything to achieve this goal. Though the public came to trust and admire the powerful California railroad moguls, in truth, they were corrupt business-men and ruthless bosses.

As president of the company, Stanford's job was to court pub-lic opinion and use his political influence to raise money from county and state government agencies. By 1863, Stanford had secured millions of dollars from the state of California. The Central Pacific would transport convicts, members of the state militia, and materials for agricultural fairs for free. In return, the railroad would receive state bonds that could be sold for the company's profit. This was an important deal. Many people demanded the con-struction of the railroad, but few were brave enough to invest in it. The general opinion was that the four Sacramento store own-ers were going to lose their fortunes and their reputations as busi-nessmen in the wild peaks and deep gorges of the Sierra Nevada.

Collis P. Huntington was chosen as vice president of the Central Pacific Railroad. From his office in New York City (he had moved there after the formation of the Central Pacific, but he still owned the store in California), he sold stock and bought construction materials, including iron rails, shovels, picks, and wooden ties, which would then be shipped around Cape Horn to the end of the track. Once the construction of the railroad was under way, supplying the crews with materials to lay the track became a full-time job. Ships filled with materials were

often lost at sea. During the Civil War, the price of raw materials, such as black powder and iron, skyrocketed.

Huntington also traveled throughout the Northeast to pitch his new business to potential investors, but no one would take a chance on the struggling railroad. If completed, potential investors argued, the railroad might not see a profit for more than twenty years. In addition, the Civil War had destabilized the American economy. Paper money was often worth as little as thirty-five cents on the dollar. Huntington was forced to offer banks and investors Central Pacific bonds to secure loans. As well, he used his own investment in the company, his reputation as a businessman, and government aid that the company had not yet earned as collateral for private loans.

As a member of the board of directors for the Central Pacific, Charles Crocker established a construction contracting business called the Charles Crocker Contract and Finance Company. He then awarded his firm the job of contracting the construction of the first stretch of railroad from Sacramento to Roseville, California. Crocker's firm was responsible for hiring construction companies to build the railroad, its stations, and its warehouses, and for supplying these construction companies with all of the materials and building equipment they required. In return, the Central Pacific would pay Crocker $400,000 in cash and Central Pacific stock for the first eighteen miles of track.

The Big Four were the only stockholders in Crocker Contract and Finance. Therefore, the cash and Central Pacific stock that

Mark Hopkins was born on September 1, 1813, in Henderson, New York. He became a successful merchant on the East Coast, and, in 1849, he joined the thousands who moved west to California. Hopkins and twenty-five other New York City merchants established the New England Trading and Mining Company. When they arrived in San Francisco, the company disbanded, and Hopkins settled in Sacramento. He opened a store on K Street, just next door to Collis Huntington's store. In a disastrous fire that destroyed much of the town in 1852, both men lost their businesses and had to rebuild. Eventually, the two became partners, selling heavy equipment primarily to miners. This photograph was taken in 1865.

Crocker's firm was paid for the job was divided among them. Whatever money came into the Central Pacific coffers—from the government or from private investors—was circulated within the Big Four. Crocker's scheme was so complicated that the extent of the scam remains unclear even today. Judah was not a stockholder in Crocker Contract and Finance, and he began to fear that the Big Four, in an effort to make a profit from the railroad's construction, would drive it into bankruptcy.

In 1861, Mark Hopkins was chosen as the treasurer of the Central Pacific Railroad. He was the eldest of the Big Four and was considered the wisest of the group. Eventually, all decisions had to be approved by Hopkins. As it turned out, the construction of the Central Pacific was more complicated than anyone had anticipated. Public opinion had turned against the Big Four. Critics accused the Central Pacific of using the government funds allotted to the company by the Pacific Railroad Act to lay tracks only as far as Dutch Flat. From there, travelers would have to follow the Big Four's toll road to the Nevada mines.

Most significantly, tensions were mounting within the company. One important debate between Judah and the Big Four was over where the Sierra Nevada officially began. The Central Pacific was given more government funds for track laid over the mountain range and its foothills than for track laid over flat land. The Big Four believed it was in the company's immediate financial interest to extend the official limits of the mountain range as far west toward Sacramento as possible. Crocker arranged to have surveys taken to establish the foothills as beginning at Arcade Creek, seven miles east of the Sacramento River. Judah believed this obvious fabrication would not endear the company to lawmakers and potential investors, even though it would fund the railroad on a more immediate schedule. In addition, Judah was increasingly distrustful of the Crocker Contract and Finance scheme.

Judah and several other members of the board of directors were convinced that the Big Four had to be bought out. However, in the end, Judah could not raise the money to buy their stock and was compelled to sell his share in the company to the Big Four. Though he was still chief engineer, Judah no longer owned stock in the railroad. He made a final trip to New York to meet with investors he hoped would buy out the Big Four and save the Central Pacific from corruption and ruin. On the trip, he contracted yellow fever in Panama. He arrived in New York and died a week later, on November 2, 1863.

CHAPTER 3

THE UNION PACIFIC BUILDS WEST

The 1862 Pacific Railroad Act provided for the formation of the Union Pacific Railroad Company, to be led by 163 commissioners. These men selected Samuel R. Curtis as their temporary chairman and agreed to begin selling stock in the company at once. They were able to sell sizable interests in the company to only three men. Brigham Young, the leader of the Mormons, bought the largest share, while both Dr. Thomas Durant, who had funded General Grenville Dodge's initial surveys, and George Francis Train invested in twenty shares each.

Veteran railroad man General John A. Dix was the Union Pacific's first president, but he was eventually replaced by Oliver Ames, a shovel manufacturer from Boston. Throughout the construction of the railroad, Durant served as vice president and was the company's real leader. Like the Big Four, Durant was in the railroad

Dr. Thomas Durant, vice-president of the Union Pacific Railroad Company, poses at the end of the track on the flat plains of Nebraska in 1866. This photograph was taken to publicize the Union Pacific's completion of the track to the 100th meridian, 247 miles west of Omaha, Nebraska. To the right of the track, telegraph poles are in place. The wires were attached by a separate crew as the rails were laid. While many historians have criticized Durant for his greed and arrogance, it cannot be denied that his enthusiasm was a driving force in the construction of the Union Pacific.

business to make money, and he and George Train pioneered a great swindle in an attempt to secure a profit.

The two men bought an unsuccessful corporation based in Pennsylvania and renamed it Crédit Mobilier of America. They sold over $300,000 in stock in the company. The Union Pacific, under Durant's orders, awarded construction contracts to Crédit Mobilier and paid the company in cash. Crédit Mobilier, or rather Durant, used the money to buy Union Pacific stocks and bonds at face value and then sold them for an inflated price on the open market or used them as collateral to secure loans.

By selling the stocks, Crédit Mobilier could make a huge profit even if the Union Pacific never laid a single rail. However, by rewarding its investors with huge annual dividends, Crédit

Like all other towns along the Union Pacific railroad, Laramie, Wyoming, began as a hell-on-wheels town, the name given to the dirty, dangerous communities that were established at the end of the track as it headed west. In May 1868, only two weeks after the rails had been laid through the town, the *Cheyenne Frontier Index* newspaper claimed that Laramie maintained a population of 2,000. This promotional photograph, which looks down an empty B Street toward the rickety Union Pacific Hotel, illustrates the dusty, makeshift life that existed at the end of the track.

Mobilier and the Union Pacific were always on the verge of bankruptcy. Like the Central Pacific, the Union Pacific begged and borrowed for money to build the railroad. Chief engineer Grenville Dodge was constantly suspicious of Durant's greed, and to protect Crédit Mobilier, Durant constantly questioned Dodge's authority. However, despite the disagreements between the company's vice president and its chief engineer, the Union Pacific built a railroad in record time.

The railroads employed thousands of men who broke through uncharted wilderness and laid timber and iron ties at the speed of a walking horse. On any given day, laborers were scattered on either side of a 200-mile-long line. They built the railroad in waves, each crew performing a particular task with speed and precision. Using picks and shovels, men known as graders were the first crews to follow the line the surveyors had marked out with wooden spikes. The graders carved cuts, filled ravines, and cleared the roadbed of vegetation, rocks, and trees. Hundreds of thousands of cubic yards of earth were carried in or hauled out using an army of handcarts pushed by men or pulled by horses.

When they reached the mountains, the graders used black powder and nitroglycerin to blast through miles of rock and to carve tunnels out of solid granite and limestone. A path of earth two feet high and twelve feet wide was scraped and padded down with heavy steel plows pulled by oxen or horses. The grade was packed by hand with stone ballast or sand. The next crew laid the ties—between 2,260 and 2,640 per mile of track. Then came the men who laid the rails.

Horse-drawn wagons traveled along the track, each carrying about forty rails and an appropriate number of spikes and chairs (pieces of iron that supported the rails on the track). The wagons would stop just before the end of the line, and five men would gather on either side. Then, two men would raise one end of a rail, and three men would seize the other end, guiding it as it slid out of the wagon. Each rail weighed about 700 pounds. The chairs were put in place by another gang of men. When the foreman shouted "Down!" the men carrying the rails dropped them into place. A man known as the gauger would kneel down to check the distance between the two parallel rails. When instructed, the laborer known as the spiker would pound in a spike with a loud blow from his sledgehammer. Two parallel rails were laid every thirty seconds, and the mighty ring of the sledgehammer sounded like clockwork.

A group of Pawnee warriors poses in front of a Union Pacific passenger car in October 1866. The car is an elegant Pullman Palace Sleeping Car that was purchased by Thomas Durant to carry a group of politicians and reporters on a tour from Omaha to the end of the track, 247 miles west. The Pawnee were invited to entertain the tourists. In Columbus, Nebraska, the Pawnee rode through the railroad camp on horseback, their faces and bodies covered with war paint. The frightened tourists were assured that it was a show put on for their enjoyment. Late into the night, the Pawnee performed war dances and staged a battle for the crowd.

Not long after the sound of the sledgehammer faded, the company carpenters arrived. They built stations, warehouses, and offices on the land granted to the railroads by the government. Towns were laid out with care by railroad supervisors, and lots were sold at auction to newly arrived settlers.

The work crews were followed by a band of several thousand nomadic bartenders, gamblers, prostitutes, thieves, and confidence men (con men). Each night, they built temporary towns of tents and clapboard buildings in the open fields along the railroad or on the outskirts of the company towns. They catered to the rowdy railroad workers, mostly young men who were far from home and who had a steady income.

The towns at the end of the track were known as hell-on-wheels towns. They averaged one murder per day, and their residents were universally criticized as a "congregation of scum" (as travel writer Samuel Bowles puts it in Stephen Ambrose's *Nothing Like It in the World*). Many hell-on-wheels towns, like Benton, Wyoming, disappeared after the railroad moved on, leaving behind only a small cemetery. Others, like Cheyenne, Wyoming, which General Grenville Dodge considered one of the worst places he had ever seen, survived and flourished. Wood-frame houses replaced the canvas tents, and honest businessmen settled in the community. Slowly but surely, the railroads drew people west, and towns grew on the dusty, alkali plains of Wyoming.

Westward settlement flourished at the expense of North America's Indian populations. In 1862, Congress ratified the Homestead Act, which granted every United States citizen the right to claim 160 acres of land in the western frontier. The central plains, soon to be connected to both coasts by rail, were flooded with eager settlers. Towns grew, and farmers cultivated the land where buffalo had once grazed, causing the buffalo herds to starve.

As the railroad stretched across the country, dividing it north from south, it also interrupted the seasonal migration of the buffalo, who would not cross the tracks. In addition, the railroad men found sport in shooting buffalo and leaving their carcasses to rot. By the end of the nineteenth century, the buffalo, which had been the foundation of the Indian economy for generations, were nearly eliminated. Plains Indians, including the Sioux and Cheyenne, attempted to defend their land and way of life from the whites and the railroad, which was a powerful symbol of white expansion. War parties attacked the railroad camps, stole horses and oxen, destroyed supplies, and killed laborers and train passengers. Telegraph poles were torn down, wooden track ties were removed or burned, rails were undone, and trains were run off the mangled tracks.

In response, the U.S. government employed Pawnee warriors to defend the railroad camps and the growing white settlements from hostile tribes. The Sioux and Cheyenne referred to the Pawnee as "Hang Around the Forts," suggesting that they were willing pawns in the hands of whites. However, the Pawnee were longtime enemies of the Sioux and Cheyenne, and the Pawnee warriors enjoyed their work and the safety provided by the U.S. government. The army supplied the Pawnee with food, clothing, money, and the newest Springfield rifles.

Nonetheless, even the U.S. military was not equipped to protect the settlers or railroad laborers at every moment, so General Grenville Dodge insisted that every man working on the railroad be armed. When armed, the Union Pacific laborers—mostly well-trained Civil War veterans—were able to defend themselves. As a general in the army and chief engineer of the railroad, Dodge played a part in the destruction of the Plains nations. The Indian population quickly dwindled, and their traditional way of life came to an end. Ultimately, the Indians were forced to either live on government-organized reservations or risk death in the new West.

CHAPTER 4

CARVING OUT THE SIERRA NEVADA

The Central Pacific continued to cope with an unreliable supply of materials, a rowdy workforce, and a concerned but enthusiastic public. Materials were shipped greater distances every day as the track entered the isolated peaks and canyons of the Sierra Nevada. The gangs of adventurous young men who had signed on for the job in Sacramento quit once the railroad reached the promising gold fields of eastern California, where they dreamed of striking it rich. The Big Four were left with a fraction of their workforce and no local population from which to hire. In the spring of 1865, they needed 5,000 men and had only 800. Charles Crocker suggested that they hire fifty local Chinese laborers.

This photo shows the camp of the Chinese laborers. It is dated between 1868 and 1869. The Chinese employed by the Central Pacific were considered odd by their white counterparts. While the white laborers lived on beef and beans and drank the cold water of nearby streams, the Chinese laborers imported dried oysters and fish and exotic fruits and vegetables, including bamboo shoots and seaweed. They drank only lukewarm tea. The Chinese also bathed every day in warm water. These habits were considered womanly by the white laborers (who might have bathed as infrequently as once a week), but they kept the Chinese healthy and strong.

The Chinese had come to California in the same flood of immigration that had brought Stanford, Crocker, and Hopkins to the West Coast. Nearly 60,000 young Chinese men had dreams of striking it rich in the gold mines, but there were many obstacles in their way. They were bullied and often robbed when they approached the large mines; therefore, they worked primarily on smaller, less profitable mines. Unlike their white counterparts, they were forced to pay a miner's tax, a permission tax, and a water tax. They were also taxed for hospitals, property, and public schools, which they were not allowed to attend. They were not allowed to obtain citizenship or to testify in court. They were regularly robbed, beaten, or killed by their employers and rival miners. In 1858, the California legislature passed a law prohibiting their immigration, but they continued to come.

Stephen Ambrose reports in *Nothing Like It in the World* that when Crocker suggested hiring Chinese workers, James Harvey Strobridge, the Central Pacific's superintendent of construction, replied, "I will not boss Chinese!" The Chinese were considered weak and unmanly. Strobridge eventually relented but gave the Chinese the relatively simple task of filling horse-drawn carts with rubble. The Chinese were so hardworking in this and every subsequent task they were given that the Central Pacific came to depend on them for their most dangerous and labor-intensive jobs, while the skilled work of masonry, carpentry, and laying rail was reserved for white laborers.

The Chinese workers, usually led by Irish bosses, were hired to dig trenches and fill gaps, cut down trees, and carve out tunnels by hand. They were originally hired at $28 per month (about $304 today) but were soon paid $31 per month (about $336 today). Their sleeping quarters were provided for, but not their

As the Central Pacific Railroad carved its way from Sacramento to Promontory Summit in Utah, it was necessary to cut fifteen tunnels through solid granite cliffs—a task that had never before been attempted. Most people thought it was impossible. The longest of these tunnels was number six, shown here. It cut through the Sierra Nevada summit at Donner Pass. The Donner Pass was named after the ill-fated Donner Party. This group of frontier settlers had attempted to cross the mountain range in the winter of 1846. They were snowbound in the mountains and were eventually driven to cannibalism to avoid starvation. Forty-one of the eighty-nine-member group died; the remaining forty-eight lived to tell the story. This incident cast a dark shadow over the mountains and anyone foolish enough to attempt crossing them. This photo dates from 1867.

food. By the end of 1865, the Central Pacific employed more than 7,000 Chinese laborers and only 2,000 white laborers.

The army of Chinese laborers faced their most difficult task in the fall of 1866, when they began work on the Summit Tunnel. The Summit Tunnel was the sixth tunnel on the road from Sacramento. It cut through a peak of the Sierra Nevada 7,017 feet above sea level. The tunnel was 1,659 feet long. Initially, the men attacked the granite wall from either side, but eventually, they cut a ninety-foot-long shaft down into the rock from the top. Laborers were lowered into the shaft in baskets and worked from the inside out in both directions while another crew of laborers worked from the outside in.

Narrow holes were made with hand drills. The laborers packed black powder into the holes, lit the fuses, and shouted a warning. The men on the outside would run as far away as possible, while the men in the shaft were quickly lifted out in baskets. Once the explosion was over and the smoke cleared, the men went back to pick away at the rock.

Four hundred men drilled away at the Summit Tunnel in eight- or nine-hour shifts twenty-four hours a day. Each day, they made less than a foot of progress on each face. As the winter of 1866–1867 approached, the snow accumulated in drifts of up to thirty feet. That year, there were forty-four storms in the Sierra Nevada peaks. The Chinese were forced to carve tunnels in the snow that led from their camps to the work site. Windows and chimneys were cut in the walls of snow to provide a glimpse of the sky. The workmen lived in a maze of tunnels under the snow for many months.

An untold number of men died in the construction of the Central Pacific. Many were caught in the black-powder explosions or buried alive under an avalanche of rock or snow. Sometimes, their bodies were found when the snow melted the following spring, their shovels and picks still tightly clutched in their hands. When winter set in, food and other supplies were not regularly delivered, and the laborers faced starvation. The wind howled, and the camp was bitterly cold. The men continued to pick away at the granite face for over a year, completing the tunnel and laying the rails by November 1867.

CHAPTER 5

BRIGHAM YOUNG AND THE MORMONS

Before the arrival of the Union Pacific Railroad, Nebraska and Wyoming were considered part of the Great American Desert. The land was dusty and inhospitable. It was miserably hot and dry in the summer and bitterly cold in the winter. After the railroad route left the North Platte River, there was no water. There were no hardwood trees to make wooden rail ties. All of the materials had to be shipped by steamboat along the Missouri River and by rail from Omaha to the end of the track.

Just as the Union Pacific had crossed the desolate border between Nebraska and Wyoming, the Central Pacific penetrated the Summit Tunnel. According to the Pacific Railroad Act, the company that laid the most rail the fastest received the most money and the largest share of land grants. The directors of both companies were willing to go to any length to finish first, but they were just as likely to cut corners to save time and money. Consequently, parts of the railroad were poorly constructed or

A group of tracklayers poses on a handcar along the Union Pacific tracks in Echo Canyon, Utah, less than ten miles east of the 1,000-mile mark. This photograph, from around 1869, was taken by A. J. Russell, who documented the construction of the Union Pacific.

simply left unfinished. The track, laid on an uneven and unstable grade, curved sharply and climbed steep inclines. The wooden bridges and snowsheds were fire hazards. The ties were made of a brittle wood that would need to be replaced in three years' time.

The Union Pacific sped through Wyoming, laying up to four miles of track in a single day. They made it well into Utah by the end of 1868. On January 9, 1869, the Union Pacific had laid 1,000 miles of track west of Omaha, Nebraska. The railroad had conquered the Great American Desert. Nearly bankrupt and facing a desperate labor shortage, they began the last leg of the race.

The Mormon settlement in Salt Lake City, Utah, was in many ways self-sufficient. Before the arrival of the railroad, it was the only white settlement along the Platte Valley route between the Sierra Nevada and Omaha, Nebraska. The Mormons were primarily farmers until the spring of 1868. That year, thick swarms of grasshoppers had descended on the fields of central Utah, destroying the crops and, with them, the economy. Farmers were forced to abandon their fields, leaving thousands of young men in need of work.

On May 6, 1868, Thomas Durant sent an urgent telegram to Brigham Young, the leader of the Mormon Church. Durant asked Young to assemble a crew of laborers to make the grade from Echo Canyon, Utah, to the Great Salt Lake, and to name his price. Young had an interest in the completion of the railroad and was eager to have the two tracks meet in Salt Lake City. He believed the railroad would bring manufactured goods, religious converts, and tourists. He instantly agreed. While the Union Pacific tracklayers were approaching the Utah border from the east, the Mormons went to work leveling a grade for about $2 per day each.

The Mormons proved to be skilled and reliable workers. They carved the frozen ground during the day and cleared the rubble by

The Mormon Church was founded by Joseph Smith. After his assassination in 1844, the small but earnest congregation was led by Brigham Young. Young and a community of followers moved west to escape religious persecution, eventually establishing the settlement of Salt Lake City, Utah, on the southern end of the Great Salt Lake. The church sent missionaries back to the northeastern United States and to England, where they converted people to Mormonism and encouraged them to join the community of the faithful in Utah. Wagon trains of converts followed the original Platte Valley route, and the population of Salt Lake City grew steadily. As these song lyrics by G. W. Anderson suggest, many Americans were very hostile toward the Mormons and were particularly resistant to the Mormons' practice of polygamy. In the song, Anderson vows to track the Mormons all the way to Salt Lake City, beat them, and force them to live by the laws and customs of the majority of Americans. This lyric sheet dates from around 1860.

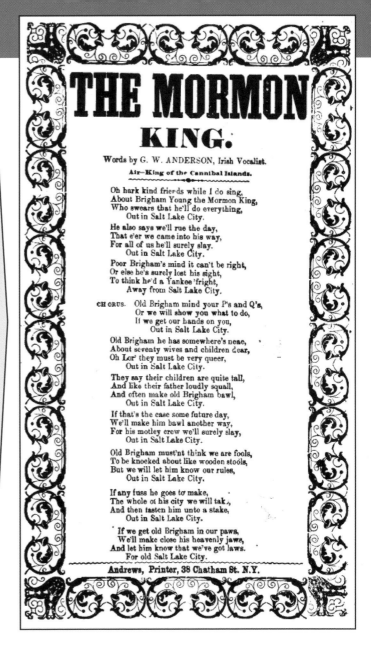

the light of brushfires at night. Unlike the hell-on-wheels towns, the Mormon camp was quiet and safe. The Mormons didn't drink, gamble, or engage in violent behavior, and the Union Pacific officials agreed that they were ideal employees. Durant, however, refused to pay them. Instead, he paid the Union Pacific stockholders, himself included, 300-percent dividends on their investment that year, and therefore did not have the money to pay more than half of the Mormon workforce. Durant was running the Union Pacific into the ground, and the board of directors was eager to get rid of him.

CHAPTER 6

THE GOLDEN SPIKE

It was agreed that the Central Pacific and Union Pacific railroads would meet at Promontory Summit, Utah, thirty-seven miles north of Promontory Point, which looks down on the northern end of the Great Salt Lake. A crowd gathered to witness the historic event. Four companies of the 21st Infantry and an army band joined the commotion. A golden spike was cast and given to the railroads by San Francisco contractor David Hewes. Weighing just over fourteen ounces, the solid gold spike would be placed in a preexisting hole and ceremonially tapped into place by Central Pacific president Leland Stanford. A telegraph wire was connected to the spike. When they made contact at noon on May 10, 1869, the sound of the event would be instantaneously reported across the country.

Thomas Hill's painting *The Last Spike* (from around 1881) is frequently reproduced. However, it is not a true depiction of the event. For example, Theodore Judah, who had died nearly six years before, is pictured next to Lewis Metzler Clement, his successor, and Charles Crocker—both of whom were not in Utah on the day of the ceremony. Collis P. Huntington, pictured behind Leland Stanford, was in New York, and Mark Hopkins was in California. In one very important way, the painting and its legend differ. In the painting, two Chinese laborers crouch on the track behind F. L. Vanderberg, who holds the golden spike for Stanford to hammer into place. An Indian stands to the right of the crowd and gazes forward. Considered unimportant at the time, these figures are excluded from the people represented in the legend of the painting. They represent the many nameless laborers and American Indians who lost their lives as the railroad stretched across the country.

KEY TO THE PORTRAITS.

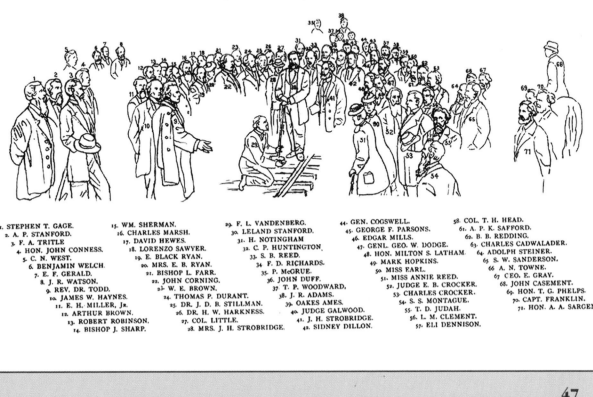

1. STEPHEN T. GAGE.
2. A. P. STANFORD.
3. F. A. TRITLE.
4. HON. JOHN CONNESS.
5. C. N. WEST.
6. BENJAMIN WELCH.
7. E. F. GERALD.
8. J. R. WATSON.
9. REV. DR. TODD.
10. JAMES W. HAYNES.
11. E. H. MILLER, Jr.
12. ARTHUR BROWN.
13. ROBERT ROBINSON.
14. BISHOP J. SHARP.

15. WM. SHERMAN.
16. CHARLES MARSH.
17. DAVID HEWES.
18. LORENZO SAWYER.
19. E. BLACK RYAN.
20. MRS. E. B. RYAN.
21. BISHOP L. FARR.
22. JOHN CORNING.
23. W. E. BROWN.
24. THOMAS P. DURANT.
25. DR. J. D. B. STILLMAN.
26. DR. H. W. HARKNESS.
27. COL. LITTLE.
28. MRS. J. H. STROBRIDGE.

29. F. L. VANDENBERG.
30. LELAND STANFORD.
31. H. NOTINGHAM
32. C. P. HUNTINGTON.
33. S. B. REED.
34. F. D. RICHARDS.
35. P. McGRUE.
36. JOHN DUFF.
37. T. P. WOODWARD.
38. J. R. ADAMS.
39. OAKES AMES.
40. JUDGE GALWOOD.
41. J. H. STROBRIDGE.
42. SIDNEY DILLON.

44. GEN. COGSWELL.
45. GEORGE F. PARSONS.
46. EDGAR MILLS.
47. GENL. GEO. W. DODGE.
48. HON. MILTON S. LATHAM.
49. MARK HOPKINS.
50. MISS EARL.
51. MISS ANNIE REED.
52. JUDGE E. B. CROCKER.
53. CHARLES CROCKER.
54. S. S. MONTAGUE.
55. T. D. JUDAH.
56. L. M. CLEMENT.
57. ELI DENNISON.

58. COL. T. H. HEAD.
61. A. P. K. SAFFORD.
62. B. B. REDDING.
63. CHARLES CADWALADER.
64. ADOLPH STEINER.
65. S. W. SANDERSON.
66. A. N. TOWNE.
67. CEO. E. GRAY.
68. JOHN CASEMENT.
69. HON. T. G. PHELPS.
70. CAPT. FRANKLIN.
71. HON. A. A. SARGENT.

Two trains, the Central Pacific's Jupiter and the Union Pacific's Number 119, faced each other on the tracks. After several speeches, the final wooden tie, made of laurel, was brought forward and put in place. Dr. Thomas Durant gave one tap on the last spike, and Stanford prepared to finish the job. Stanford swung his hammer and missed, instead striking the iron rail. Indistinguishable from the real thing over the telegraph wire, it was announced that the spike had been hammered into place and the telegraph report was subsequently cut. Bells were rung around the country, and everyone began to celebrate. The Jupiter and the Number 119 moved toward each other until their noses nearly touched. Then both trains separated, and each was ceremoniously pulled over the final rail in turn. The job was done.

The words "The Last Spike" are carved on the head of the golden spike pictured on the next page. On one side of the five-and-five-eighths-inch-long shaft are the words "The Pacific Railroad, ground broken Jany 8th 1863; completed May 8th 1869," referring to the original date planned for the final ceremony. Another side reads "May God continue the unity of our Country as the Railroad unites the two great Oceans of the world." Carved in the remaining two sides are the names of the officers of the Central Pacific and Union Pacific railroad companies.

For the Big Four, Durant, Dodge, all their investors and employees, and all of the Americans who eagerly followed the story as it unfolded in their local newspapers, the saga of the transcontinental railroad was not yet over. Durant still had not paid Brigham Young for the grade between Echo Canyon and the Great Salt Lake, a job that had begun nearly a year before. With the Union Pacific virtually bankrupt, Durant was forced to pay Young in nearly $600,000 worth of railroad equipment. Young was eager to

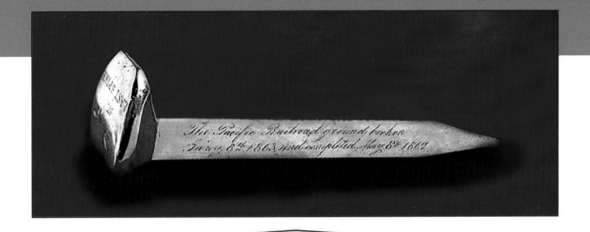

While the final laurel tie was reduced to a twig by souvenir scavengers, the golden spike was rescued after the ceremony and returned to Leland Stanford. Today, it is housed in the Stanford University Museum of Art in Palo Alto, California.

get into the railroad business himself, and the Mormons quickly built a successful spur between Ogden, Utah, and Salt Lake City. Only weeks after the golden spike was hammered in, Durant was voted off the Union Pacific's board of directors, and he left the railroad business for good.

In 1872, the *New York Sun* broke the story of the Crédit Mobilier and corruption within the railroad companies. The United States House of Representatives investigated allegations against Crédit Mobilier and the Central Pacific and Union Pacific railroads. It became clear that the men who ran the railroads had profited immensely from the enterprise by bribing and cheating the government, exploiting their labor force, and ignoring debts they incurred along the way. Perhaps not accidentally, however, the Central Pacific's records had been lost in a fire. The Union Pacific, despite overwhelming proof of its corruption, was given only an official censure from the House of Representatives. America's first national corporations had escaped investigation essentially unharmed. Dodge and the Big Four worked for the railroads for the rest of their lives, and their names became legendary in the business.

CHAPTER 7

RIDING THE RAILS

Once the last rail was laid, passengers could travel from New York to San Francisco in seven days. There were three classes of cars: first, second, and third, or emigrant, class. As the railroad expanded, the price decreased, making the journey even more accessible to everyone. In 1870, passengers paid $136 (the equivalent of about $1,477 today) for first-class passage across the country. They rode, slept, and dined in elegant Pullman cars outfitted with the comforts of home. That same year, $110 (roughly $1,194 today) would buy a second-class ticket across the country, and for just $65 (about $705 today) a traveler could go by emigrant car.

Trains were sometimes caught in winter storms in the Sierra Nevada and were forced to wait out the bad weather at the nearest station town. With decreasing frequency, the cars were attacked by Native Americans, most of whom had either been killed or moved to reservations. Still, the railroad was the safest and fastest way to travel long distances, and in the days before highways and automobiles, the romance of the open rail captivated the American imagination.

While first-class passengers enjoyed the refinement of a Pullman sleeper, third-class, or emigrant, passengers sat on stiff wooden benches. The emigrant sleeping cars were named for their passengers, the floods of newcomers trying to make a life in the United States. The 1884 blueprint shown on the next page is annotated by the Central Pacific's second chief engineer, Lewis Metzler Clement: "Designed and first built at the Sacramento Shops of the C.P.R.R."

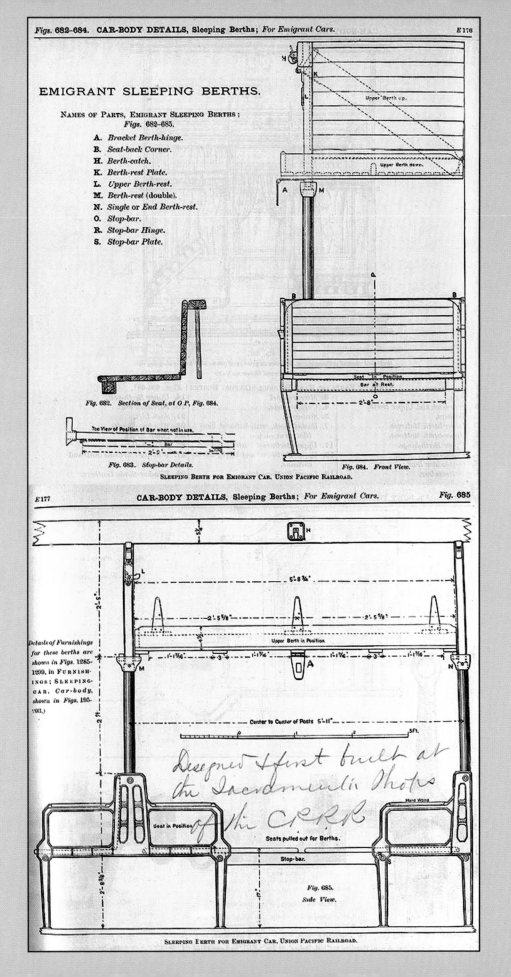

EMIGRANT SLEEPING BERTHS.

NAMES OF PARTS, EMIGRANT SLEEPING BERTHS; *Figs.* 682–685.

A. *Bracket Berth-hinge.*
B. *Seat-back Corner.*
H. *Berth-catch.*
K. *Berth-rest Plate.*
L. *Upper Berth-rest.*
M. *Berth-rest (double).*
N. *Single or End Berth-rest.*
O. *Stop-bar.*
R. *Stop-bar Hinge.*
S. *Stop-bar Plate.*

Fig. 682. Section of Seat, at O P, Fig. 684.

Fig. 683. *Stop-bar Details.*

Fig. 684. *Front View.*

SLEEPING BERTH FOR EMIGRANT CAR. UNION PACIFIC RAILROAD.

E 177   **CAR-BODY DETAILS,** Sleeping Berths; *For Emigrant Cars.*   Fig. 685

Details of Furnishings for these berths are shown in Figs. 1285–1299, in FURNISHINGS; SLEEPING-CAR. Car-body, shown in Figs. 195–203.)

Fig. 685.
Side View.

SLEEPING BERTH FOR EMIGRANT CAR, UNION PACIFIC RAILROAD.

The engine pictured on this stamp (issued in 1869) may have been the Central Pacific Railroad Company's engine Jupiter, which attended the final golden spike ceremony at Promontory Summit, Utah, the year the stamp was issued. The Jupiter was powered by burning wood. The large, round structure at the top of the smokestack was a cover with a wire screen to catch burning embers and prevent fires. A coal-burning engine, such as the Union Pacific's Number 119, had a straight smokestack.

Throughout the construction of the railroad, local newspapers chronicled its every step. Stories of Indian attacks frightened readers, tales of corruption and scandal shocked them, and details of the project's unprecedented progress roused their patriotism. The country was gripped by, as one railroad official described it, "railroadmania." Proof of this came in the unlikely form of new postage stamps.

Before 1869, every stamp issued by the United States Post Office displayed a portrait of George Washington, Benjamin Franklin, Thomas Jefferson, Andrew Jackson, or Abraham Lincoln—the elder statesmen of American independence. In 1869, the Post Office broke the mold. Two three-cent stamps were issued that illustrated a new era of American patriotism. One shows a Pony Express rider on horseback, celebrating the overland mail service that was by then out of business. The other stamp (above) shows a gleaming, wood-burning railroad

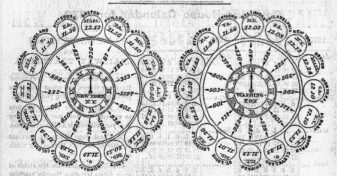
From the beginning, railroads depended on punctuality. To make sure the trains ran on schedule, the railroad companies invented Standard Railway Time in 1883, which created the four North American time zones still in use today. The continent was divided into Eastern, Central, Mountain, and Pacific zones, and railroad timetables like this one took the zones into account. Passengers could plan their trips by locating their point of origin and their destination on the timetables. With the advent of the national rail system, a vast expanse of wilderness was harnessed, and time itself was tamed. These documents date from 1883.

engine. Smoke billows from its smokestack as it chugs across an open field. The train was the new symbol of American freedom.

It may be difficult to appreciate the courage and genius required to build a railroad stretching 1,774 miles through uncharted wilderness. Theodore Judah, Grenville Dodge, the Big Four, and Dr. Thomas Durant led an army of 20,000 men into the wilderness and changed America forever. The transcontinental railroad ushered in a new era of communication, social progress, and cultural diversity, as ideas and products traveled as quickly as a telegraph signal or a speeding train. It did so at an exceptionally high price, however, for this new era dawned at the expense of the immigrant laborers who had worked the rails and the Indians who had fought against the railroad revolution. In the end, like many great human accomplishments, the building of a transcontinental railroad signaled the beginning of one era and the end of another. It was an unprecedented act of creation and a force of horrible destruction. We can only marvel at its construction and wonder what the world might be like had it never been done.

PRIMARY SOURCE TRANSCRIPTIONS

Page 15: NATIONAL REPUBLICAN PLATFORM ADOPTED BY THE NATIONAL REPUBLICAN CONVENTION, HELD IN CHICAGO, MAY 17, 1860.

Resolved, That we the delegated representatives of the Republican electors of the United States, in Convention assembled, in discharge of the duty we owe to our constituents and our country, unite in the following declarations:

The Republican Party.

1. That the history of the nation during the last four years, has fully established the propriety and necessity of the organization and perpetuation of the Republican party, and that the causes which called it in [omitted word] existence are permanent in their nature, and now, more than ever before, demand its peaceful and constitutional triumph.

Its Fundamental Principles.

2. That the maintenance of the principles promulgated in the Declaration of Independence and embodied in the Federal Constitution, "That all men are created equal; that they are endowed by their Creator with certain inalienable rights that among these are life, liberty and the [omitted, two words] that to secure these rights, governments are instituted [omitted, two words] deriving their just powers [omitted word] the preservation [omitted word] and shall be preserved.

[Omitted word] Union.

3. That to the [omitted word] the States, this nation owes its unprecedented increase of population, its surprising development of material resources, its rapid augmentation of wealth, its happiness at home and its honor abroad and we hold in abhorrence all schemes for Disunion, come from whatever source they may: And we congratulate the country that the Republican member of Congress has uttered or countenanced the threats of Disunion so often made by the Democratic member without [omitted word] and with applause from their political associates; and we [omitted word] those threats of Disunion, in case of a popular overthrow of their ascendancy as denying the vital principles of a free government, as an avowal of contemplated treason, which it is the imperative duty of an indignant People sternly to rebuke and forever silence.

State Sovereignty.

4. That the maintenance inviolate of the Rights of the States, and especially the right of each State to order and control its own domestic institutions according to its own judgment exclusively, is essential to that balance of power on which the perfection and endurance of our political fabric depends; and we denounce the lawless invasion by armed force of the soil of any State or Territory, no matter under what pretext, as among the gravest of crimes.

Sectionalism and Democracy.

5. That the present Democratic Administration has far exceeded our worst apprehensions, in its measureless subserviency to the [omitted word] of a sectional interest, as especially evinced in its desperate exertions to force the infamous Lecompton Constitution upon the protesting people

of Kansas; in construing the personal relation between master and servant to involve an unqualified property in persons; in its attempted enforcement, everywhere, on land and sea, through the intervention of Congress and of the Federal Courts, of the extreme pretensions of a purely local interest; and in its general and unvarying abuse of power entrusted to it by a confiding people.

Its Extravagance and Corruption.

6. That the people justly view with alarm the reckless extravagance which pervades every department of the Federal Government; that a return to rigid economy and accountability is indispensable to arrest the systematic plunder of the public treasury by favored partisans; while the recent startling developments of frauds and corruptions at the Federal metropolis, show that an entire change of administration is imperatively demanded.

A Dangerous Political Heresy.

7. That the new dogma that the Constitution, of its own force, carries Slavery into any or all of the Territories of the United States, is a dangerous political heresy, at variance with the explicit provisions of that instrument itself, with contemporaneous exposition, and with legislative and judicial precedent; is revolutionary in its tendency, and subversive of the peace and harmony of the country.

Freedom, the Normal Condition of Territories.

8. That the normal condition of all the territory of the United States is that of Freedom: That as our Republican fathers, when they had abolished slavery in all our national territory, ordained that "no person should be deprived of life, liberty, or property, without due process of law," it becomes our duty, by legislation, whenever such legislation is necessary, to maintain this provision of the Constitution, against all attempts to violate it; and we deny the authority of Congress, of a territorial legislature, or of any individuals, to give legal existence to slavery in any Territory of the United States.

The African Slave Trade.

9. That we brand the recent re-opening of the African Slave Trade, under the cover of our national flag, aided by perversions of judicial power, as a crime against humanity and a burning shame to our country and age; and we call upon Congress to take prompt and efficient measures for the total and final suppression of that execrable traffic.

Democratic Popular Sovereignty.

10. [Omitted word] the recent vetoes, by their Federal Government of the sets of the Legislatures of Kansas and Nebraska, prohibiting Slavery in those Territories, we find a practical illustration of the boasted Democratic principle of Non-Intervention and Popular Sovereignty embodied in the Kansas-Nebraska Bill and a demonstration of the deception and fraud involved therein.

Admission of Kansas.

11. That Kansas should, of right, be immediately admitted as a [omitted word] under the Constitution recently formed and adopted by her people, and accepted by the House of Representatives.

Encouragement of American Industry.

12. That, while providing revenue for the support of the general government by duties upon her imports, sound policy requires such an adjustment of these imports as to encourage the development of the industrial interests of the whole country; and we commend that policy or national exchanges, which secures to the working men liberal wages, to agriculture remunerating prices, to mechanics and manufacturers an adequate reward for their skill, labor, and enterprise, and to the nation commercial prosperity and independence.

Free Homesteads.

13. That we protest against any sale or alienation to others of the Public Lands held by actual settlers, and against any view of the Free Homestead policy which regards the settlers as paupers or suppliants for public bounty; and we demand the passage by Congress of the complete and satisfactory Homestead Measure which has already passed the House.

Rights of Citizenship.

14. That the Republican party is opposed to any [omitted word] in our Naturalization Laws or any State Legislation by which [omitted, two words] of citizenship hitherto accorded to [omitted word] from [omitted word] shall be abridged or impaired, and in favor of giving a full and [omitted word] protection to the rights of all classes of [omitted, three words] whether native or naturalized, both at home and abroad.

River and Harbor Improvements.

15. The appropriations by Congress for River and Harbor Improvements of a National character, required for the accommodation and security of an existing commerce, are authorized by the Constitution, and justified by the obligation of Government to protect the lives and property of its citizens.

A Pacific Railroad.

16. That a Railroad to the Pacific Ocean is imperatively demanded by the interests of the whole country that the Federal Government ought to render immediate and efficient aid in its construction; and that, as preliminary thereto, a daily overland Mail should be promptly established.

Co-operation Invited.

17. Finally, having thus set forth our distinctive principles and views, we invite the co-operations of all citizens, however differing on other questions, who substantially agree with us in their affirmance and support.

# GLOSSARY

alkali Salty; related to the composition of the soil.

ballast A heavy material used to secure or improve the stability of an object or construction.

black powder A chemical explosive made of potassium nitrate, charcoal, and sulfur.

bond A document issued by a government or company that promises the payment of an amount of money at a certain time in the future.

broadside A large poster or printed advertisement.

chair A piece of iron that supports the rails on a railroad track.

collateral A security on a loan, something that is offered by the borrower to protect the investment of the lender.

Confederacy The thirteen Southern states that formed a separate and independent nation during the American Civil War.

converts People who change their religious views or join a religion.

delegates Representatives for a person or group of people.

dividends Shares of profit.

foreman The leader of a work crew.

grade The level land on which the ties and rails are laid.

hell-on-wheels town A town that grows at the end of a railroad track as it is being built.

immigrant Someone who comes to a country to live permanently.

laurel A kind of evergreen tree.

level An instrument used to establish a horizontal line that is used in surveying and construction.

locomotive A machine that is moved by the power of an interior engine.

lode A deposit of a mineral.

manifest destiny A future event accepted as inevitable; in the mid-nineteenth century in the United States, a policy of expansion and colonization.

mogul A great figure in business.

Mormon A member of the Church of Jesus Christ of Latter-day Saints.

nitroglycerin A chemical explosive, more volatile than black powder.

platforms Written declarations of an individual's or political party's principles and beliefs.

ravines Narrow, steep-sided valleys.

roadbed The flat surface on which the ties, rails, and ballast of a railroad track are laid.

schooner A large, two-masted sailboat.

seceded Broke away from.

snowshed A long, wooden structure that covered the railroad tracks in the snowy peaks of the Sierra Nevada.

spur A railroad track that branches off from the main track.

stagecoach A small carriage drawn by horses.

stock Certificate of part-ownership in a corporation.

summit The highest point.

surveyor A person who determines the contour of land using mathematical calculations.

telegraph A machine that communicates via coded signals relayed by electrical currents traveling over wires.

ties Long pieces of wood into which railroad rails are spiked.

Union The collection of states that remained part of the United States during the American Civil War.

yellow fever An infectious disease common in the Tropics.

FOR MORE INFORMATION

Due to the changing nature of Internet links, the Rosen Publishing Group, Inc., has developed an online list of Web sites related to the subject of this book. This site is updated regularly. Please use this link to access the list:

http://www.rosenlinks.com/psah/trr/

FOR FURTHER READING

Ambrose, Stephen. *Nothing Like It in the World: The Men Who Built the Transcontinental Railroad*. New York: Simon and Schuster, 2000.

Beebe, Lucius. *The Central Pacific and the Southern Pacific Railroads*. Berkeley, CA: Howell-North, 1963.

Howard, Robert West. *The Great Iron Trail: The Story of the First Transcontinental Railroad*. New York: GP Putnam's Sons, 1962.

McCague, James. *Moguls and Iron Men: The Story of the First Transcontinental Railroad*. New York: Harper and Row, 1964.

BIBLIOGRAPHY

Ambrose, Stephen. *Nothing Like It in the World: The Men Who Built the Transcontinental Railroad*. New York: Simon and Schuster, 2000.

Beebe, Lucius. *The Central Pacific and the Southern Pacific Railroads*. Berkeley, CA: Howell-North, 1963.

Chinn, Thomas W., H. Mark Lai, and Philip P. Choy, eds. *A History of the Chinese in California*. San Francisco: The Chinese Historical Society of America, 1969.

Howard, Robert West. *The Great Iron Trail: The Story of the First Transcontinental Railroad*. New York: GP Putnam's Sons, 1962.

Huffman, Wendell W. "Iron Horse Along the Truckee: The Central Pacific Reaches Nevada." *Nevada State Historical Society Quarterly*, Vol. 38, No. 1, Spring 1995, pp. 19–36.

Huffman, Wendell W. "Railroads Shipped by Sea." *Railroad History*, Bulletin 180, Spring 1999, pp. 7–30.

Kraus, George. "Chinese Laborers and the Construction of the Central Pacific." *Utah Historical Quarterly*, Vol. 37, No. 1, Winter 1969, pp. 41–57.

McCague, James. *Moguls and Iron Men: The Story of the First Transcontinental Railroad*. New York: Harper and Row, 1964.

Steiner, Stan. *Fusang: The Chinese Who Built America*. New York: Harper and Row, 1979.

Warman, Cy. *The Story of the Railroad*. New York: D. Appleton and Company, 1998.

INDEX

# PRIMARY SOURCE LIST

Page 9: Advertisement in *Rochester Daily Advertiser* for W. R. Andrews, 1849. Housed in the Library of Congress. Created by *Rochester Daily Advertiser*.

Page 11: Map by surveyor William Jarvis McAlpine showing the best railroad routes to the West, 1853. Housed in the Geography and Map Division, Library of Congress.

Page 12: Major General Grenville M. Dodge of the Union army. This photograph was taken between 1860 and 1865. Housed in the Brady National Photographic Art Gallery, Library of Congress.

Page 15: Advertisement for the National Republican Convention, which was held in Chicago on May 17, 1860. Housed in the Chicago Press & Tribune Office. Created by the Chicago Press & Tribune.

Page 19: Theodore Judah, chief engineer of the Central Pacific Railroad. This portrait was painted by C. E. Watkins in 1863. Housed in the Central Pacific Railroad Photographic History Museum.

Page 22: Leland Stanford, president of the Southern Pacific Company railroad. This portrait was painted circa 1880.

Page 24: Photograph of Collis P. Huntington, who made his fortune selling mining equipment to travelers on their way to California in search of gold.

Page 25: Portrait of Charles Crocker, who was an investor in the Central Pacific Railroad. Housed in the California State Railroad Museum in Sacramento.

Page 26: Photograph of Mark Hopkins taken in 1865.

Page 29: Photograph taken in 1866 of Dr. Thomas Durant. Housed in the Union Pacific Railroad Photographic Archives.

Page 30: Photograph taken in 1866 of Union Pacific Railroad workers. Housed in the Union Pacific Railroad Photographic Archives.

Page 31: Photograph taken in 1868 of downtown Laramie, Wyoming, in its early, boomtown years. Housed in the Central Pacific Railroad Photographic History Museum.

Page 33: Photograph taken 1866 of Pawnee warriors before a Union Pacific Pullman Palace Sleeping Car. Housed in the Central Pacific Railroad Photographic History Museum.

Page 37: Photograph taken in 1868 or 1869 of a camp of Chinese laborers who worked for the Union Pacific Railroad. Housed in the Central Pacific Railroad Photographic History Museum.

Page 39: Photograph taken in 1867 of Tunnel Number 6, the longest of the tunnels that passed through the Sierra Nevada summit at Donner Pass. Housed in the Central Pacific Railroad Photographic History Museum.

Page 43: Photograph taken in 1869 by A. J. Russell of Union Pacific tracklayers in Echo Canyon, Utah, less than ten miles east of the 1,000-mile mark. Housed in the Central Pacific Railroad Photographic History Museum.

Page 45: Lyrics to the song *The Mormon King*, written by G. W. Anderson in 1860. Housed in the Rare Books and Special Collections Division, Library of Congress.

Page 47: *The Last Spike*, painted in 1881 by Thomas Hill. Housed in the California State Railroad Museum in Sacramento.

Page 49: Photograph of the Golden Spike. The spike is housed in the Stanford University Museum of Art in Palo Alto, California. Manufactured by the William T. Garrett Foundry.

Page 51: Blueprint of the Pullman emigrant sleeping car created by Lewis Metzler Clement in 1884. Housed in the Central Pacific Railroad Photographic History Museum.

Page 52: Three-cent stamp from 1869 with illustration of the Central Pacific Railroad Company's Jupiter locomotive.

Page 53: Railroad timetables created in 1883 that exemplify the newly established Standard Railway Time. Housed in the Central Pacific Railroad Photographic History Museum.

About the Author

Gillian Houghton is an editor and freelance writer living in New York City. Her most recent railroad trip took her from New York's Pennsylvania Station to her hometown of Milwaukee, Wisconsin. She plans to traverse the western half of the country by rail soon.

Photo Credits

Cover, pp. 22, 24, 25, 29, 30, 31, 33 © Hulton/Archive/Getty Images; pp. 19, 39, 43, 47 (top and bottom), 49, 51, 52, 53 (top and bottom) © Central Pacific Railroad Photographic History Museum; pp. 9, 11, 12, 15, 45 © Library of Congress; p. 26 © California State Railroad Museum Library; p. 37 © Corbis.

Editor

Annie Sommers

Design

Nelson Sá